Once the Smudge is Lit

Kegedonce Press, 2023

Copyright © by Kelsey Borgford and Cole Forrest
December 2023

Published by Kegedonce Press
11 Park Road, Neyaashiinigmiing, ON N0H 2T0
Administration Office/Book Orders: P.O. Box 517, Owen Sound, ON N4K 5R1
www.kegedonce.com

Printed in Canada by Trico Printing
Art Direction: Kateri Akiwenzie-Damm
Cover and inside artwork: Tessa Pizzale
Design: Chantal Lalonde Design

Library and Archives Canada Cataloguing in Publication

Title: Once the smudge is lit / poems by Kelsey Borgford and Cole Forrest.
Names: Borgford, Kelsey, author. | Forrest, Cole, author.
Description: First edition.
Identifiers: Canadiana 20230586589 | ISBN 9781928120407 (softcover)
Subjects: CSH: First Nations poetry (English)—21st century. | LCGFT: Poetry.
Classification: LCC PS8283.I5 O53 2023 | DDC C811/.60808973071—dc23

All rights reserved. No part of this book may be reproduced in any form or by any
electronic or mechanical means including information storage and retrieval systems,
without permission in writing from the Publisher. Member of Access Copyright
Sales and Distribution – www.litdistco.ca:

For Customer Service/Orders
Tel 1–800–591–6250 Fax 1–800–591–6251
100 Armstrong Ave. Georgetown, ON L7G 5S4
Email: orders@litdistco.ca

We acknowledge the support of the Canada Council for the Arts which last year
invested $20.1 million in writing and publishing throughout Canada.

Canada Council   Conseil des arts
for the Arts   du Canada

We would like to acknowledge funding support from the Ontario Arts Council,
an agency of the Government of Ontario.

ONTARIO ARTS COUNCIL
CONSEIL DES ARTS DE L'ONTARIO
an Ontario government agency
un organisme du gouvernement de l'Ontario

OPENING THE CIRCLE

Table of Contents

Poems by Kelsey Borgford

Poems by Cole Forrest

CLOSING THE CIRCLE

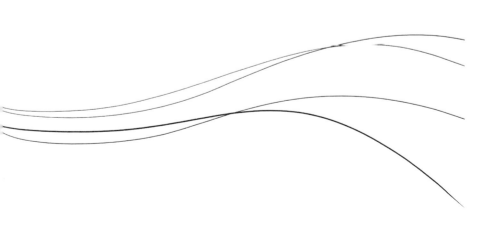

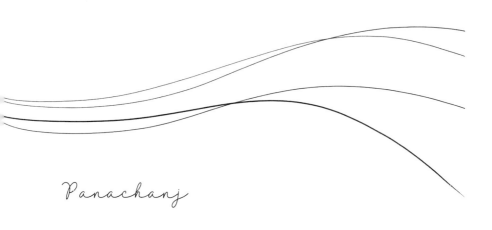

Panachanj

the porcupine came alive as she pulled at its quills

it danced one last time with her

she had magic in her fingertips

she gave meaning and enchantment to all that she touched

no matter how many quills poked through her gloves
piercing her hands
she kept her patience

bloody and broken, it didn't matter
she made it a damn beautiful thing

she always did

Nokomis Baa

i visited your grave today
and left sage instead of flowers
i spoke to you and told you

"i see you in everything
each cloud
each plant
each wave

you're here with me
dancing alongside me at the powwow
sitting beside me in the lodge
listening when I pray"

we never really stopped speaking,
i found your words etched into the moon
and i responded back by writing you into every poem

how can a person always there, and never really there at all?
they'll ask me
expecting me to not see the irony in it all
the harsh realities of life

but i'll tell them
you carry them in the sole of your moccasins
on the tip of your tongue
and in your medicine bag

knowing they're lying in the soil, but dancing in the spirit world

alive in me
and gone away forever

Nangoonhs

she felt like she was floating
even if her feet were planted firmly upon the rock below her
wet from the newly melted ice and cooled by the spring air

she flashed her light into the shallow water
hundreds of sparkling eyes shone back at her
the twinkle dancing in the soft waves wasn't too dissimilar to her own

light glowed within her that night
knowing she carried on the traditions of her family
with a spear gripped between her palms

nangoonhs,
she is her father's daughter.

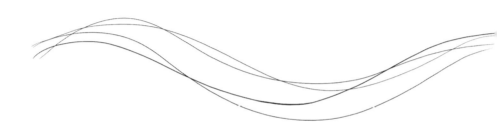

Powwow Nights

under the spotlights of the powwow, we share the summer air

we're on a fleece blanket cuddled up next to one another

keeping ourselves warm on the metal bleachers

the darkness is no match for the light we find within
   one another tonight

we throw our heads back, and our laughs echo louder than the drum

i've never seen smiles so bright

it's good to be back

i don't want these powwow nights to end

Neyaaba'aakwaang

the water rushed over me
and knocked me to my knees

the river took me with it
it didn't hurt when i held my breath;
i've been holding it my whole life

i was enveloped in the tide
from my toes to my soul
the water rushed against me
washing away all that i carried with me

the things i thought i needed to live were taken from me
with a simultaneous violence and gentleness

and when i finally dragged myself out of the current
i kissed the earth desperately

thank you,
i'm alive
i'm alive
i'm alive

Nishnaabe Boy

you were delivered from the sun
she kissed you so much on the way down your skin turned bronze

how could she not?

you are a beautiful boy
your heart holds space for ceremony

sacred fire always burning inside
giving warmth to those around you

your body is a lodge
made from the strongest willows
and the softest cedar

hair made from sweetgrass
braided with morning dew

eyes familiar and brown
like winter bark
and tobacco offerings

you're created from Nanabush stories
humble and knowing
i find safety in you

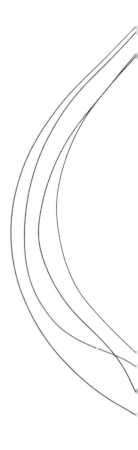

Expectations.

i swim to the bottom of the ocean
to try and recreate the world
i am tired of hurting

my fist gripped tight onto the mud
as i held my breath

sand fell through my fingers as the waves washed it away

mother earth spoke to me
she told me all that I need is already here on the surface

look a little deeper,
love a little longer

Creator's Daughter

the night i was born gokomis giizis herself came to paint the sky
she cradled me within her effervescent light
and illuminated the rolls on my body
she thought i looked so beautiful
she made sure i'd keep them forever

i am the culmination of those before me
DNA sewn together like a star quilt

a song of survival sings throughout me
the first sound in the universe began with a rattle
and ended up in my chest

i'm stitched together with resilience embedded in my seams

layers of mkwa fat coddle me
my body finds softness in the places i was forced to become hard

ancestors decorated the parts of me i love the least with meegis
shells and trade beads

i knew i was creators' daughter when he dotted me with cellulite
the same way he formed the stars in the sky
who am i not to love what she made?

Firekeeper

fell for the fire keeper

he held me close
kept me warm

danced with me tonight

we moved through ancestral planes
despite remaining in the tipi that night
two spirits bound to earth
and destined to more

we felt the beat of the drum
through our feet
and towards our hearts

he fed our fire

gonna keep his heart safe

didn't wanna admit it

but i fell for the fire keeper

Round Dance Season

it's colder than you remember it being last year
singers standing by the door, smoking canadian classics
only the finest

big blast of warm air hits you as you walk through the doors
almost as much as the sound of all the pretty girls singing

ribbons just real stacked on your skirt
beaded earrings sparkling under the gym lights
NDN country's favorite fashion show

big wave from your bro over at the snack table
before he runs off to go drum

chubby babies in their little moccs
wiggling their toes to the beat
smoked hides never been cuter

our three-hour drive was worth it
another round dance season begins

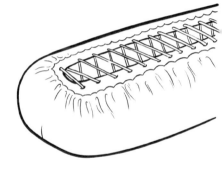

Rape Culture

it creeps in quietly through the mildew laden windows
leaving behind an incessant dark

sneaky and unanticipated
it took on the form of those you trusted

i'd heard stories of the trickster
but i never thought i'd be the one to meet him

everyone knew it was there
but like a deer in the headlights no one dared to speak

they heard it snatches the voices of those who defy
subservience helped it grow

we don't talk about that here

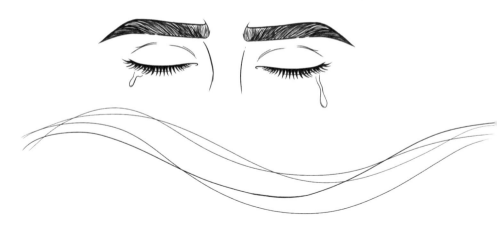

Rez Funeral

the weeping made you want to fall to your knees with grief
it echoed throughout the school gym

one of my hands held a platter of egg salad funeral sandwiches
the other gripped the tobacco in my pocket tight
my finger and thumb smoothed it into a hard ball
to distract myself from crying too

the brightly coloured florals painted on the walls gave
    no solace this time
the air stayed cold and still

maybe i could stay a little longer

Pretendian

bear walks in the bush
bear eats a fish from the river
bear climbs a tree
bear is bear

human walks in the bush
human eats a fish from the river
human climbs a tree
human is not bear

because bear learned from mother bear, and grandmother bear,
and ancestor bear
and human learned from watching bear

he decided to take, take, take all that bear had
and what made bear, bear
but even so human knows deep down
no matter how many fish he eats, he could never be bear

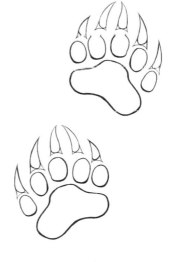

Falling In Love

you know the kind of cold,
just before snowfall
you can practically smell the moose meat cooking
your mom's old moccasins protecting your feet from the old camp floor
the world sits still for a moment

it swallows you whole if you're not careful
and it engulfed me on the midnight boat ride
but i didn't complain because a fire burned within me

surely if the light was brighter than that dim glow provided to us by the
stars dotting the sky he would see the way my cheeks blazed fiery red
maybe he would know that it didn't come from the bitter air
but rather the way he navigated the land

Moss Bag Baby

moss bag baby
swaddled in your mother's love

pressed against her body
feeling her warmth
imitating the comfort of the womb

you feel it,
you and she are one again for just a few moments longer

moss bag baby
you are at peace
the smell of home tanned hide eases any upset that might come your way

moss bag baby
she carries you on her back
keeping you as close as she can
you'll long for this the rest of your life

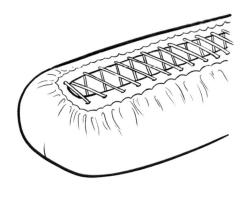

Beyond The Snow

they thought me to be a blueberry bush covered in snow
nothing to yield

my branches fragile and bent from the burden i carried
my potential stifled

none could see beyond what enveloped me
sweetness laid below

wait for summer
give me time to grow

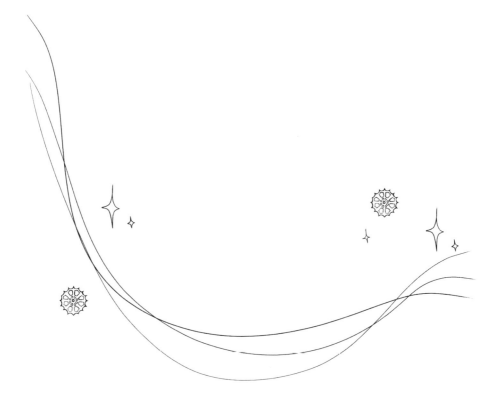

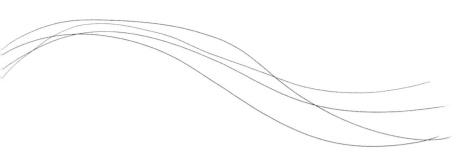

Three Generations

Nokomis baa sat at a creaky wooden table speaking
   nishnaabemowin with comfort and ease

she spoke of seemingly insignificant matters

filling the silent room with her words

she didn't know that her words would one day be revered and
   the people would yearn to hear that sort of fluency

Nokomis baa didn't teach Nimamaa the tongue she held

sometimes i wonder if it was to protect her

from bloodthirsty Indian agents and vicious schoolchildren

her uncles tried to teach her

but she never grasped the words

zhagaanashmowin filling the bones of our home

i struggle to spit the words out

we were born to speak these words

three generations ago

Across The Powwow Trail

you and i share the moonlight
but we're thousands of miles apart
still i dream of you,
and speak of you in my prayers

i'll offer a little extra tobacco
in hopes that creator brings us together
to walk our journeys together

every sunset
every sparkling lake
and every round dance song speaking of lovers
suddenly made me think of you

and yet any beautiful thing I came across
could never be as beautiful as you
and your soft smile

i long for the day we can share all the beautiful things together
like fresh ode'min and gentle love

Back to the Circle

i am a child once more,
watch me take my first steps
and stumble in my moccasin

you'll notice me miss a beat
and trip over the powwow grounds
i'll accept my missteps humbly
but i refuse to fall to my knees again

you can't take this from me anymore
i will walk forth
a fire burning in me carry's me

throw in your tobacco
and i'll dance it home to creator

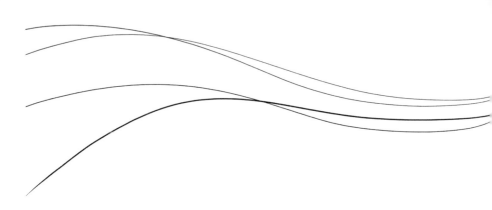

Until Next Time

i came from shining blue waters
and birch trees

and went to poplars, buffaloes,
and dusty lands
with winds that blew strong across the plains

to be with the boy who showed me home can have more than
    one meaning

until next time
i'll remember how as the night took over
he wrapped me in layers of blankets
and his arms

until next time
i'll see him in my dreams
and be with him in prayer

until next time

Water Girl

in a sea of colorful ribbons
and flashy fabrics
i only see the dancer in sumac red and cornflower blue

his moccs slide across the grass real smooth
meeting the earth with grace

his bells call to me as they shake
keeping me looking
yet my eyes never wanted to wander

watching him make his stops with ease
i knew i made the right decision
i'd chose to be his water girl every time

Whitefish Bay

beds of wild rice surround us
while dark clouds roll in,
he kisses me softly

thunder birds sound in harmony with the drum
the universe came together to write us a love song tonight

grey waves dance to the melody in the distance
as the rain starts to fall
so do i

on my way home i make an unplanned stop
at the shores of Gichigami

i make an offering
of cowrie shells and cedar branches

lowering my hands into the ice-cold waters
i ask the universe to keep singing our song

Nanabush Smiled at Me

my brown skin fades with the winter sun
wallowing inside foxholes where the fox died
I imagine a prayer in my mind for dead animals,
I don't always I mean it
I spoke with Nanabush last night Spoke the language to me
open the maple wooden door
a green blanket at your feet
the stars below your being
cosmic experiences the creator withholds
until it's time to close your eyes and sleep
but you don't really sleep when you're Indigenous
explore me, Nanabush
you don't need eyes to explore
if there's something cultural about your bones
Nanabush stood across the table
you hear so many stories about someone, then it's still the first time
you meet them language I understand but my tongue can't pronounce
I can speak the language
Nanabush laughs
what a good looking being
so beautiful for an eternity
Nanabush is kind of hot
oh my what my mother would say if she were here
sexier than Derek Miller
blushing in a birchwood box
Nanabush takes my hand
pulls me through to the other side

The Door Closed Behind Me

opened my eyes
what happened to me
you don't really wake up when you're Indigenous
I just live in the wounds Nanabush tried to heal and sew
when I split my arm open with a saw they kissed my hand and
told secrets to my blood
dripping back into the earth
my mind is the log cabin Nanabush built
grieving above the fire my community keeps

Driving Home At 2am

2 am is sacred
drove down highway 17 at that time
we shared ghost stories
there aren't too many highway lights, not every bridge has them,
    but I've been told I have good eyes

I'll look out for us

close enough to the windshield I think about what would happen
    if we crash
sometimes I imagine a deer smashing into the car, or running
    alongside it; living and dying are the same in the northern night;
    a trauma response
the road becomes red with a truck stalled on the guardrail
looked like a moose through the windshield, splattered across asphalt

ceremony is both thought and action

antlers smashed through the front window of a truck as the moose
    wriggles to pull out is an alter to every Ojibway parent who
    raised their child alone
tires soaking up moose blood is a drink in honor of the cold night
warms me up
it's 3 am
roll up yer window

Dylan

he fell

I swear you could see him
curled up there in the hand of the creator
I saw his face again lost in a frame
the sweetgrass spread for him to appreciate
the younger brother, the youngest of the four of us swept away
   by the river
taken away by the current
he was just a boy
I don't remember the last thing I said to him
I offered him his feast plate that night that was so cold,
the world was silent and blue at the stump of a tree near the church
I prayed he'd travel safe, and that he'd be okay
he'll be okay, he'll be okay
sometimes I look up at the sky and see him up there
all he needed was a hug
I hope he's enjoying his time held by the creator
they better give him a blanket at night
he fell
just as the stars sprinkled down from the midnight sky to
let me know they were making room for another piece to join
   their constellations
whenever I see the stars out
I'll see his name dance with the moon
Dylan

Pines

when I broke through the ice
and my snowshoe was stuck
cold river water rushing

all I could feel
was my cousin's presence
who died
in a similar way

one difference
was someone
witnessed him slip
and only the tall pines
saw me

My Old Man

We had chip stand once when I was in grade nine
if you ask anyone, he's a great guy good people good person
missing out on my life my old man
we lived less than ten kilometres away from each other
    for seventeen years
the only time I've heard he leaves his house is to yell at his girlfriend
my mother was right all along
she usually is in the case of native men

I've only had two interactions with my old man
One was off the side of the highway at a picnic table
    when I was fourteen
The second was this year when I read his birth certificate

I show his Instagram
to all my friends
Indigenous mortification

Fuzzy Haired Boy

we ran back from the lake together when all the adults
    were ice fishing
flew down the hill behind the house on a broken table and
    called it a sled
last time I heard
you were gone
we were kids
now you're gone
you're still alive
but you're gone
family footsteps
there's that photo of you as a kid you have your arms crossed and
    you're making a mean face
your hair was horsehair
had the temper of one too
tried to keep you here
I ran into you on the street a while back
still kids
never got why you had to be so tough
made my heart sink
indian pain
no longer kids
real problems real problems
you know what I'm saying
problems changed your fuzzy hair
now you're gone

Lucky Indian

being homeless; I sat there in the living room of the shelter reading
Alice in Wonderland I was in grade 7
An Indigenous woman sat close to me
she called me the lucky Indian

because my eyes are blue
that's the only difference we had that night

we all suffered the same
I was homeless multiple times it probably contributes
to why I grieve every morning
and why I struggle to put my clothes away at night

I can finally have my own mess
I can finally have my own mess

yeah you're broken
you feel it everyday

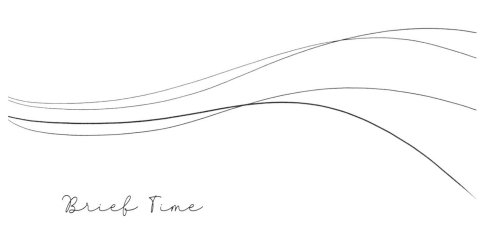

Brief Time

my body's brief time in this life
yearns for your soft skin
I'll lend you my heart
I'll melt it down and rub the oils on your chest to help you breathe again
I'll light a smudge from my heart and wash your hair in the smoke as it
plumes in the moonlight the water will see only us as we rest tangled in
this life together rest with me on the mattress
we'll make a cradleboard together we'll sew our secrets into
    the bed frame
I'll gift you my culture and love
I'll rest your head in the beaded flower
making up this body I call my being
I want you to trace your fingers on every bead
because I want you to feel what makes my skin brown and
    my eyes so blue
they've never looked so bright and it's from the glow you give
you give so much and all I want to do is reciprocate and honour you
I had a vision of a woman telling me to find something south
the southern direction is
red
spiritual
fire
warmth
my body's brief time in this life was waiting for its time
with you

Nurture/Prayer

french catholic is something I could never be wow his eyes are so blue
summer skies, I was 9 years old
two tall pine trees
scared of storms
skin is still there, in the pavement
$20 in from my grandmother, go get some chip stand
sippy cup I hid from my friends on my birthday, had a green top
chocolate milk and grilled cheese and greasy gamecube controllers
drink up, baby
a monolith to my mother's love
four seasons corner store
a slush puppy, renting 3D movies
church is unbecoming of memory
I do not go back to reminisce
a grave is a distance I can't travel

-10 am December 18th 2007-
mom opened the door closest to the kitchen
jesus christ above the hall way
home computer to the right
little boy, sitting there, dazed from sleeping on the couch a couch
cannot replace a grandmother
mom's screaming, folded grey skies
distinctly yellow eyes the night before
vague static afterwards

two moments
A partridge flew through the living room window a few years ago.
It fell right into the cabinet across the room. It was killed instantly.
There was glass everywhere. My grandfather moves from his chair.

The microburst of 2006. My mother rushing me into the bathtub to
keep me safe. Lightning had split the tree across the street in two.
A tree falls onto our street. My grandfather moves from his chair.

I don't remember Christmas that year.

It is no longer before and after, that is my mother's burden.
There is only a vintage gold watch.

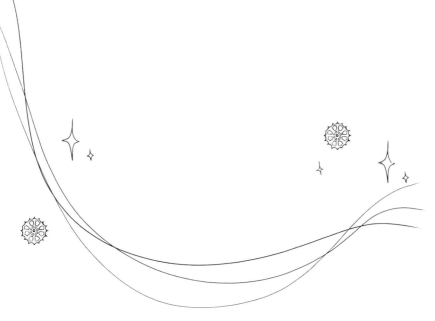

Shomis Drove The Truck Into The Ditch

My gokmis's house
just down the road from the convenience store
right off the highway
is a temple to teenage sanctuary
and elderly alcoholism
when we sit in the backyard waiting for my cousins to arrive
I feel the newest version of anxiousness
shomis drives the truck into the ditch at 2 am
but it's only 3 pm
how about a fish fry tonight?
she's already fired up the grill
a vat of vegetable oil
a low smoke point
no smoke signals here
I think every girlfriend I had in high school has sat in the gazebo
gazebo being a term for driftwood/makeshift
I remember it being a thousand degrees watching the lightning from
the front porch used to keep the doors open all night
4 am downloading mods for sims 2
gokmis's internet
somehow there's 3 different versions of the same router
staring at photos of being a little kid
passed on family members
messaging old friends from towns I use to live in
I'll come back this summer
no you won't
5 pm fish and chips is why I'm made in the creator's image
watching my figure
taking photos for my fb profile picture everyone in my school will see
another one with me in a fake smile
lots of kids do fake smiles
indigenous kids do them the best

7 pm it's dessert
sheet cake and butter tarts from sobey's
not watching my figure anymore
wooooow you eat a lot
just give it to cole he'll eat it
yeah and I ate it all
10 pm I'm playing on my cousin's ps2
looking at a journal of gta vice city cheat codes
I'm back in the room down the hall
out in the living room they're having a party jeepers
I never wondered about when it would be my time to join
because I never will
but I've heard the same siriusXM country music playlist my whole
existence which is to say I've always felt my indigeneity in some way
alright time to go home
my mom didn't drink
we both stink like smoke
2 am shomis drives the truck into the ditch
he walks out and stumbles down the road
walks up the driveway
in through the magnetized door cover
into bed.
he went into bed.

Boat Ride

getting yer boat license only takes an hour online but my mom runs
the motor for me
see you at the boat launch
Ojibway early is 5 am
Ojibway late is 6 am
fish in the summer
fish in the winter
the only difference is how drunk my relations get
what else can i say it's the fucking truth
it was true when I was kid it's true now
at my uncle willie's
I'm an adult
he's drunk and broken
used to drive me to school
used to drive the bus
my family sits around us
they're equally drunk and broken
drunk is a bottom 5 word in english
I don't apologize for drinking
but I'm sorry my family is always drunk
willie told me about being an indian working on the CNR rail a
long time ago the first time he's spoken to me
the next morning we'll be on the boat

the whole family
put them all in one dingy
and let the george jones blare
scare away the fish
drinks like a fish
fuck me, man
how bad can it get at 6 am
when you wanna reel in some pickerel
there'll be a bite
The sheepshead those ugly guys
bite my line off 20 lb line
fish all you want!
MNR nowhere
we're here
I'll hold all the faces of everyone in my family at once
and let the water fill up the boat
we've already done it to our livers the night before
it's called a natural progression
culturally we let life take its course
but I've never filled my mouth up with lake water
and felt a buzz
I only feel like the creator's giving me too much
shomis pulls up 8 pickerel
hoolaaay
he only has to put back 2 because he cares about lake repopulation
my mom pulls up 2
she's okay with it
gokmis pulls up and everyone laughs
they can hear ya from the shore ever loud you
my cousins wish they could reel in as much as me
and I don't even fish much
gifts I reject
trickster behaviour
my gokmis says what everyone's thinking about

fuck why you gotta go and ruin it
she didn't, but it's what my uncle willie says
shomis uses his quick wit and we boat back
I've never felt more like my mom
how many fish is that?
throw it all in the cooler
it's only 8 am
on the rez I've seen 8 generations pass by in an hour
the sun burns away the alcohol
uncle willie's still drinks
every time I see him I feel a new kind of broken
get yer boat license, baby bear
alright, mom
I'd carry all of you
if it meant we could have a family
and not just relations

Vision and Reflection

I woke up on a grassy plain with a tall wooden house, the only
one for a country mile. I was pulled forward to the tall door of the
house. The handle to the house was made of bone. When I opened
it, there were all kinds of n8ve people there, they were all distinct.
They sat around speaking to each other, grabbing food, cleaning up,
running up and down the stairs. I was experiencing what home felt
like for the first time. I took a seat at a table with one chair by the
window. No one acknowledged my presence walking through the
house. This is what it feels like to be normalized. I looked through
the window and there were people playing in the field. Closer to
the house was a woman dressed in a black cloak. She moved me
from sitting by the window to standing right beside her. She had
a medicine wheel made of a white substance on the ground. The
women took her cane and pointed east, then south on the circle.
She gifted me a hand drum. She gave me a song; one I hadn't heard
before. It was almost as beautiful as a fawn wood song. I sang it
with her. She pointed to the south point on the medicine wheel
again. I found myself back in the house staring from the window.
The woman took her hood off.

I don't spend every night going to bed hoping to return to a vision
everyday right now is a form of envisioning and re-envisioning
I am falling through the front porch of my gokmis's house
dogs barking tied to the front lawn
it's more dead grass than living spirit
I'll be back soon

Sturgeon Photo

In a boat in the middle of the lake
he points in every direction
all of this, is your community
I didn't hear what you said
all of this, is your community
your community, is all of this
I've never had anyone describe it to me like this before
170 years ago they farmed sturgeon for their eggs from the lake
put them in a can and called it industry
When I pick up an eagle feather on a island
I also found blueberries
I've never seen a sturgeon
Someone else called this their home
But they don't understand why that's simply not true
Sturgeon understand territory
A boat where the rip cord is pulled by my mother
    understands territory
The guy yelling from the bush asking for a 2-4 from me after asking
    him to stop his chainsaw for
a sec understands territory
the bent basketball rim at the high school understands territory
the four directions
All of this, is your community

Gen-Z Indigenous Self Portrait

I wake up with the morning sun because
I'm not putting up a sheet to cover
the light I need to shine on me
the night before I broke open
my ancestors tried to comfort me in
the backseat of an uber just keep at this pace
baby I have so many feelings for you
and the bones poking out of your closet
they should be in a museum next to the regalia
I wept when I saw a tikinagan in a space that felt like
A graveyard I went home and felt the presence of
every child's spirit you held my hand and Ojibway
flowers appeared on our palms maybe you could be
the reason to cover the big window in my bedroom I could get real
rez in the city for you the dreamcatcher on the door will catch every
time we have angry sex and turn it back into a garden love when
I look at Man Changing into Thunderbird by Norval Morrisseau
I feel a lump in my throat it could also be I
never told you about the time I began to fly
when I was 6 when my mother's boyfriend
at the time held me by the hands spun me and
flung me onto the ice my body slid a few feet
and my body laid there lifeless on the ice
my body lifeless is not death it was precursor
to where I was going to be at every day this year
I cup an abalone shell when I light the smudge
this is how I need to you to hold me trauma
is not the only thing I fall apart from and the morning my great
grandmother died

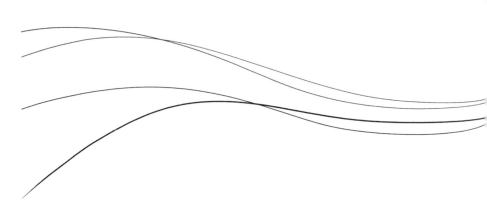

was a long sword through my 9 year old heart my
shomis used to line the grass with gasoline leading up to the
fire pit and when everyone would sit down he'd
take a match to it all and he'd laugh so hard
I wish you could see how bright the flames were and how bad the
bugs were
the next morning when we'd get McDonald's come eat with me
sweetie forget about the charcoal that line my cheeks from every
time I
was gaslit by my mother's boyfriends don't call me your boy
friend we're something more is there a word in your
language for it honey whisper it at 3am when my dreams are
loud pull me back into this bed I'm staying browner longer can you
please call me your sacred boy and we'll tongue kiss at 6am after
you tell me I've been snoring brush your teeth with me and
it smells like sweet grass when you smile at me
you are a trickster and I am an eagle it's the way we
laugh and love in the morning sun.

Art's Lane

maybe we could have a better life
than just sitting on the side of the road
watching the moose travel down the hill
mother moose baby moose
screen door banging against the door frame
it was my gokmis's house at one point
now it's ours
now my cousin lives there
inherited
yeah that's the old fire pit
one morning I woke up there were dead groundhogs strewn
    across the yard
abbey just wanted to play
even though she had a sister
I don't know where those dogs went
if I asked my mom now, I wouldn't want to know the answer
there was a drifter that came by looking for trouble
my mother hid me behind the door
her fiancé and I would download music off lime wire and
    eat mcdonald's
parent child bonding
my mother hid me behind the door
we slept in tents in the backyard one night
there were so many shad flies as the sun came up
I'd hear so much fighting
trying to play computer games
one time I accidentally killed a moth and I cried all afternoon
when I saw the baby moose walk away with mother moose
It's all I'd ever wanted
us to walk away

Come Over Here!

We will travel to this place
With our beings
With our hearts
With our little stars
The water will embrace you, it is my ancestor
For 9000 years we have lived in this lake
Our love medicine will give them another generation
As children of the sun, children of the water

Gokmis

Oh Gokmis
I love you
Even when you resent us
Don't want anything to do with us Oh Gokmis
You don't have to be so tough rest your eyes
Let us make you a ribbon skirt
Oh Gokmis

Someone who watches

I smudged every day for a week smudging was embarrassing to me
washing my hair in front of everyone then the smoke plumed

whispered for me to keep going
I was afraid to smudge in the circle but not while my ancestors
watched there's something so post-modern

about being a chronically online n8tve

that doesn't want to show their face but would open a portal to the
cosmos just to look the creator
in the face
and say place me here, I want to be with you forever, baby
and the creator would move stars for you
hold you in their big hands
I saw your ig post
that's a weird fucking subreddit babe
who's yer internet provider? I'm yer provider!
I'll call you
someone who watches

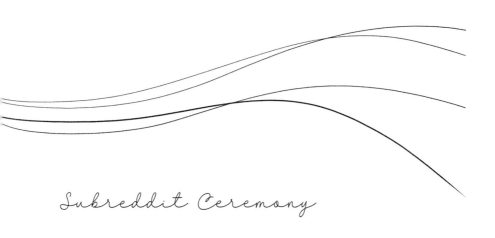

Subreddit Ceremony

your dark living room lit by laptop light at 1:30 am is a ceremony
only if you're indigenous
c'mon show me yer status card

jkjkjk

you don't need a status card
to creep the indian country subreddit
just enough sense of community
to know the previous generations
are looking at the same posts

Smelts :)

my mom taught me how to cook so I give my body fish
and my ancestors laugh with joy we sing the same songs

one of the best days of my life
was finding smelts at the grocery store
smelts are small fish you put in a batter and fry in oil

not trying to be that way I suppose you put every fish in oil and batter

batter being flour and salt
a little bit of work with my hands
we always put our fish in batter and oil
when I heat up the pan I'm always afraid I'll start a fire
I caught wild smelts once when I was a kid
my cousin clinton
caught them

take their little guts out
rinse with cold water
enjoy

Chiefly

Maybe I'll be chief one day
When I'm some kind of old dog
When I'm finally thoughtful
When I'm some kind of adult
When are you both Indigenous and adult?
When are you both thoughtful and Indigenous?
When are you both an old dog and Indigenous?
When are you both Indigenous and maybe
When I'm some kind of whole
When I'm finally compassionate
When I'm some kind of cultural pillar
When are you both compassionate and a cultural pillar?
When are you whole and compassionate and indigenous?
When are you an old dog and a cultural pillar
    and compassionate and chief?
When are you Indigenous and maybe I'll be old one day
    when I'm some kind of chief
When I'm finally whole

Our Great Grandfathers and Their Chairs

two moments

A partridge flew through the living room window a few years ago.
It fell right into the cabinet across the room. It was killed instantly.
There was glass everywhere. My grandfather moves from his chair.

The microburst of 2006. My mother rushing me in to the bathtub
to keep me safe. Lightning had split the tree across the street in two.
A tree falls onto our street. My grandfather moves from his chair.

He lays beside my grandmother in the ground
I heard so many things about him
Even lived with him
There's a photo with a shadow on his face
My mother told me things
I saw

He passes away 6 months after

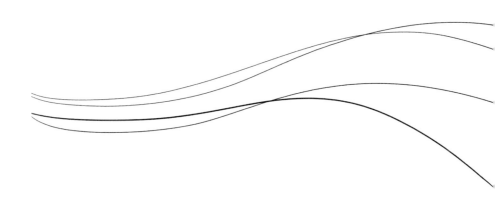

Zizaagi'in

Indigenous love
is two broken things, picking up the pieces of each other
fish oil from frying fish the night before
the medicines burning in the morning
this is also cultural knowledge
how many tipis reeked like sex
my apartment is a box set on the corner of a street named
     after a great chief
it rains
the contents of the box reveal themselves, a little indian with
     a toy drum
the people quickly rush by
this is it what it's like in the city
until another indigenous person notices
and picks up the box takes it home, dries you off
gives you a new drum
plays with you
indigenous love
is a stack of boxes filled with cultural artifacts
cultural artifacts being cheap furniture and players light cigarettes
a breeze calmly makes its way into the room
everything falls over
the cigarettes light and everything burns
it's not every time
but it's almost every time
let's just lay here for our own sakes
don't label it
let's just listen to each other
touch my shoulder, your hand is cold, it's getting cold outside
     eh let's warm up
Indigenous love is a coat you got at a thrift store you wear to get tea
     at the cafe with the one other person from your rez that lives here
I don't want to
let's just hold each other

put my liver back
sow my heart back into my body
I'll breath marrow back into your bones
and place traditional secrets under your finger nails
whisper what I told you to
the words I taught you in my language
Indigenous
love
is

Anishinaabe Love Poem

in my dreams
come into my dreams
I dream sleeping beside you my life partner
lay with me
under stars
my stars your stars
when we make love
I'll kiss your belly
I care for you
under sun
moon
we make love under the moon rest my love
rest with me
I love you

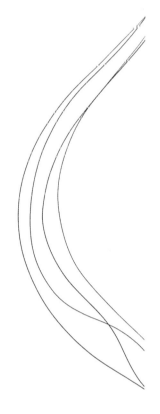

Spirit

I answered auntie's MSN message

-10 am December 18th 2007-
mom opened the door closest to the kitchen
jesus christ above the hall way
home computer to the right

mom's screaming, folded grey skies
distinctly yellow eyes the night before
vague static afterwards

I changed the time on your watch
from 6:30 pm to 7:00 pm
time passed
while I carry you with me

Things I don't talk about

french catholic is something I could never be
blue eyes
brown hair
scarred my arm
scarred my face

grey hair in a gold vial
I sat on the bed and dropped one on the floor
you were still there

Momma Migizi

I saw my mother from afar
she kept walking farther and farther away

my mother calls from our community
how's about a fish fry when you're back

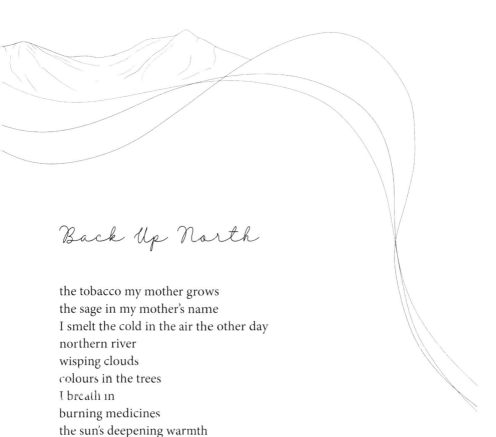

Back Up North

the tobacco my mother grows
the sage in my mother's name
I smelt the cold in the air the other day
northern river
wisping clouds
colours in the trees
I breath in
burning medicines
the sun's deepening warmth
my mom

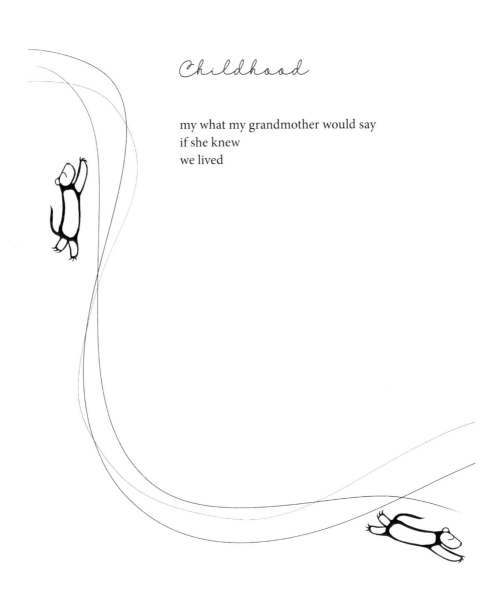

Childhood

my what my grandmother would say
if she knew
we lived

The Eagle's Nest

there's a size 3 Jordan show box of photos from the early 2000s
photos from my mother's childhood
photos of my great-grandmother
photos of my gokmis
photos of my cousins
photos of my auntie
photos of me
photos of where we lived
photos of where we travelled to
a newspaper clipping of the explosion that happened when
grandma was a child
she always walked with a limp

my mom always laughs when I pulled it out to show people
it's what happens when trauma and memory feed through
the same needle

I always tell the story of when I was 3 I sprayed lysol into my eyes
while my mom was in the shower

I remember picking up the roller coaster tycoon disc for our pc
when we moved into our upstairs apartment

Miss Cheechoo came to say hello before JK

I cried when we watched Armageddon with Bruce Willis because
I thought volcanos were possible in Nipissing

there was a volcano at one point but I didn't know that at
3 years old

we fold memories into our present
in the apartment I lived in when I was in high school

Southern Love

our love fills the hearts of all our relatives
I was a closed Nishnaabe floral before the sun in your eyes drew
    my beaded petals open
from your lips, a ceremony of honey poured onto my flower
sweet and sticky as a lay my cheeks against your thigh
I trace roses and lilacs and poppies in your lips
a ceremony of syrup
softer and kinder in my throat than any sugar bush back home
we kiss, the water from my home territory rises and splashes
    against the shore
the water pulls away comes back, pulls away, comes back
I will always come back to you

our love is the birch bark we harvest laying on the earth
crackling in the flames we huddle close to
every twinkle in our eyes is our ancestors smiling so brightly
    back at us under moonlight
our bodies entangle a smudge pluming from our rolling hips
burning cedar inside our bodies
we hold hands so tightly pressed into the dirt pictographs of
    our love appear on our palms
making love is ceremony with you

Closing The Circle

fall away, fall away
all the ashes from our smudge

the water from our beautiful faces
medicine drips onto our moccasins and skirts and hides

how many stories did we tell this time only creator and
   our grandmothers know
gonna have to chop more wood tobacco bowls emptied

plumes of feathers and smoke rise
as our heads do
from under the protection
of home and ceremony and teaching and warmth and laughter
I'll see yous, I'll see yous

For Nipissing,
our community,
our home

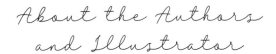
About the Authors and Illustrator

Kelsey Borgford

Kelsey Borgford is a Nbisiing Nishnaabekwe from the Marten clan. She is an emerging author, passionate about utilizing writing as a tool to revitalize cultural connections. After losing her Gokomis-baa in 2014, Kelsey sought out a means of connection with her grandmother and found that connection to her through the arts. Kelsey's work aims to pass along cultural traditions and identity. Her work is predominantly centered in the practice of beading and writing. She has a children's book, What's in a Bead, forthcoming from Second Story Press. In all aspects of her creativity, Kelsey draws inspiration from her culture, her mother, her community, and relatives in the natural world.

Cole Forrest

Cole Forrest is an Ojibwe filmmaker and programmer from Nipissing First Nation. They have written and directed independent short films that have been screened at film festivals including imagineNATIVE, TQFF, and the Vancouver International Film Festival. Cole is a recipient of the Ken and Ann Watts Memorial Scholarship and of the James Bartleman Indigenous Youth Creative Writing Award. They were the 2019 recipient of the imagineNATIVE + LIFT Film Mentorship and a 2020 Artist in Residence as a part of the Sundance Native Filmmakers Lab. Cole has supported programming at festivals including TIFF, imagineNATIVE, and Fabulous Festival of Fringe Film. They are a graduate of the Video Design and Production program at George Brown College. Cole is currently writing their first feature film. They are grateful to represent their community in all artistic pursuits.

Tessa Pizzale

Illustrator Tessa Pizzale is a Moose Cree
Indigenous Artist located in North Bay,
Ontario. She is currently working on
her Bachelors of Fine arts at Nipissing
University. Tessa creates work pieces through
digital and art pieces. She also works on
creating leather regalia belts.